FEAR OF CHANGE

RASHMI SINHA

Old No. 38, New No. 6
McNichols Road, Chetpet
Chennai - 600 031

ISBN 978-1-64899-466-1

To my readers

Contents

Acknowledgements

vii

The journey of this book from beginning to finishing point was grueling is an underestimation of the foremost degree. Even though the analysis, evaluation, exploring and recording of the data was on me singlehandedly. Getting a time was an essence of excursion.

I owe my friends and colleagues in completion of this book and above all, I must thank my parents who has been at my side through all my studies, made sure that time was unfilled and has not once conceded me to distrust my proficiencies.

CHAPTER I

Introduction

As a human, we are enduringly petrified of alterations or new changes in our life for the reason that we can't antedate the aftereffect. To overcome those fear, we need to revolutionize the result by altering our approach to tackle difficulties or grasping incidents taking place in our lifespan. In psychological study, the fear of change or changing things is named Metathesiophobia. Openly speaking, fear when reached to its greatest ridge replaces human's preference to survive. Due to fear people inclines to dwell in the past memories and put up with dejection and misery. The new change taking place in person's life occasionally frightened them and generates reluctant mindset, which correspondingly started mirroring in their behavior. Fear of change can callously influence one's career and private existences too. Fear take birth, in the core of extreme circumstances, can influence an individual's outlook to distinct surroundings in which fear exhibit. Responses to such changes comprise a sequence of biological, functional, and psychological ups and downs, that change a human's life.

In this book, we will see how a colossal change in life is alarming and exhilarating equally to many parents in the form of Empty nest syndrome, midlife crisis. Boomerang generation etc. In today's generation family (Including both parents) want to be tangled in each other's life. While couples deal with many changes and fears a lot. As a family, at first, they are anxious about having children, men exclusively have their personal distinctive uncertainties allied to work life balance and at end both (Mother and father) are reciprocally alarmed of their children growing and then getting separated from them. The temperament of dread, fear, anxiety or distress may modify in response to individuals' age-linked and inborn physiognomies, in addition to the mixture of exasperation.

CHAPTER II

Empty Nest Syndrome

Every parent hopes their lone dream to get fulfilled, they forever yearn for their kids to grow up and turn into a leading light. However, parents time and again feel abandoned or desolated, friendless, deserted and sometimes isolated, whilst their children move off. The aforementioned is an interim epoch in lifespan that emphases lonesomeness and create vandalism in life. Parents however, continually buoy up their progenies to flourish. Conversely, this episode is a lot nostalgic or psychosomatically stimulating. Countless researchers proposed that many times, parent's misery leak out and take a shape of heavy drinking habits, arguments, quarrels or separation in a house. This is called empty nest syndrome. On the other hand, various findings conclude, the new alterations in life also deliver some advantages to parents in countless aspects. It stretches a wing of new hope, gives a chance to reboot their life and start fresh. In which there is no worries to meet other's expectations, you can live a burden less life.

Maria was a mother of two children. Her kids were all grown up and last week they left for higher studies. In the starting phase, she assumed it would be pleasing to finally have a relaxing time away from all the domiciliary work. She considered to join some social service organization, which regrettably she stopped after her pregnancy and by no means get the time to rejoin.

Like Maria, the majority, when their children reach the legal age, are thrilled, because it's like they get the house all to themselves after many years. It is a heartbreaking moment but many parents try to overlook them. Momentarily, in many cases as their children go away, their mind and soul start suffering with agonizing emotion of solitude and seclusion. As a result, it befitted into an exceedingly substantial problematic course for them.

After Maria's kids left, she joins the bordering NGO and began working there. She was developing herself to get acclimatize with a neoteric routine but come what may, she felt powerless to acclimate the latest transformation in her life. At times, she gets nightmares and is confounded for sending her kids faraway. Her husband George, has also begun meeting his old friends and spend most of his time outside hanging with them. She and her husband only come across each other at dinner time and there is minus interaction between them but the best part is, they still have their dinner together. She has got no one to share her feelings freely. Earlier, at dinner table, there was lot of brouhaha, which she ostracized the utmost but now when she ponders bout those days, it makes her exultant.

The empty nest disorder is excruciating, and it embroils feelings like distress and uneasiness. To live on and cope with such circumstance, parents frequently stumble on fascinations to self-cure and block the fissure their humanity is fronting. The utmost familiar is people getting addicted to alcohol, turning into a dopehead stoner and spending less time at home with family. This human state is blemished and it is not only prejudicial but also toxic for other relations. At this point, it is imperative for parents to engage themselves in new and productive leisure interest to fill the gap. If it became a new reality and interest of their lifestyle, the emptiness in heart for their children produced can be covered with newly unearthed bliss. For this, you are required to explore and find your hobbies and interest, which you must have neglected in the course of lifespan.

After few weeks, Maria observed George changed behavior towards her, she was cheesed off with George obliviousness, she concluded to talk to him and ask for clarification. George was a great father and husband. He was overall a great man. She knew George always desired to discover the world but due to his profession and kids, he was inept to put across his interest. She also realised, he feels isolated when she leaves for work. That's why, he goes outside and stay with his friends, drinking and playing pokers. She not once wanted such bad transformation in her family, she has always cherished George and her kids. She knew what is best for all of them that's why she decided, it is the best time for her and George to go on a trip and revel in. This trip will not only give them some lone and peaceful time to talk but also refresh their mind. Chiefly, for George to come out from his dark hole. Subsequently, having this in mind, she decided to probe her husband today night.

Both of them were having dinner and George as usual was eating silently but occasionally turning his head towards TV watching news channel. The one voice communicating filled the silent room was from the female reporter delivering the news.

Not to wait more, "Hey George", Maria uttered anxiously squinting at him.

"Yes, Marie"', he responded. Maria knew, he always calls her Marie, when he is either not interested or when he's unhappy.

"Uh, I... I was thinking, let's go on a tour!". Listening her words, George eyes turned wide and he nippily turned off the TV.

"But, why...I mean, is everything alright, Maria? Out of the blue, you are mulling over to go somewhere?" He asked dubiously inspecting her with hawk eyes.

There was a deadly pause in the room. Both of them were scrutinizing each other awaiting one of them to speak.

Not to fall more into the quietness, Maria determined to speak with a fresh smile pasted on her face. "Yeah...everything is good. I'm only feeling to relish some fresh air and go someplace far. You see it's useful for health and most notable, we haven't visited any place since several years", she said genuinely.

"Okay, it's wonderful you planned to enjoy but what about your job? You have joined recently; your impression will be bad on others?" he suspected.

"George", she uttered politely resting her palm on his. "It is manageable, I've already talk to them and have given the resignation." Saying this her eyes were casted down on her plate, as if seeking for some exquisite diamonds. She does not want to debate any further on this matter, she only wants George's consent to go. She recognized this is beneficial for both. Still in his worst condition her husband is thinking of her reputation made Maria's eyes filled with tears of respect and love.

George was stunned taking note of everything his dear wife revealed just now. He always aspired to go and see the world but he was ham-fisted to express his fascination to Maria after his children left. The moment, he chose to confer this with her, he stopped himself, seeing her happy doing social work. when their kids left, he underwent the anguish of loneliness alone. He has not even gripped himself properly from the loss, Maria's statement of joining work broke him from inside. George needed her the most but he also knew her unfulfilled dream that's why he encouraged her to join. In all of this he does not know how his own life started sinking into the dimness hades. It took only one phone call from his old chums and his grieve started tormenting.

Glimpsing her wife sitting quietly in front him, gazing at him eagerly, he offered a humble nod. "Fine, let's decide where we are going? Both of their eyes were filled with contentment and hopefulness.

If we see, there are countless articles on how couples get distanced from each other or split up, when the children grown-up and they leave the house of their parents. Both of them reason, there is not anything left in the relationship because their kids were the only joining factors or linkage, who crafted the loved ones together. *"If the shackles are conked-out, birds are at liberty to fly"*. Figuratively speaking, I accept it true that this is the rightest time of life of human relationship. When two couples started as a stranger at first, they continued collectively and remained together for so many years, there has to be a touch of diminutive similarity in them. They simply need to do is discover it on their own and revitalize the fondness. At times, it also ensues your companion become extremely occupied in office work or their individual life and they overlooked your difficulty. They may perhaps be uninformed of overall experiences; it is your responsibility to disclose your complications with them and not condemn other. When we picture George character, he withholds his feelings and keep mum in front of Maria. To make her contented, he smoothly gave up his aspiration although it was not the fairest way out. He had better disclose his emotional state and resolved the dilemma. Else, his disorder would have gone saddest if Maria would not have observed. On the other side, Maria's act was of true acquaintance, her spousal support to George clasped their bond in devotedness. Spousal support genuinely helps out in such alteration in life.

George was fond of arts and collecting them is his hobby. He has collection of arts like - Poster Buon Pastore, Poster Augusto di Prima Porta and many more. Going to Rome and visiting Vatican museum was his dream come true. He was enthusiastic throughout the entire journey. Sighting George happy, Maria felt gratified. She can see the youthful version of George, jubilantly chatting with her, enlightening her with every minutiae of arts. Maria knew, she'll never be repentant going to Rome with her husband.

When humans fall in depression, they start losing interest in everything. Their life goal from tip to toe get twisted inside and they never take an effort to come out of the abyss of darkness. In such circumstances, it is also suggested to take some counselling sessions and release your grief in front others. It supports in stimulating a required psychological-behavioral transition in individuals.

Jack was the father of only child, Mia. Mia, requested to study abroad and applied in NYU. Last week the, result was declared and she was selected. Jack was also wishing the best for his daughter but he does not realize, seeing her off at the airport would be extremely painful. He confessed to his wife; he cannot imagine her daughter going far away from him. He cries his eyes out in the whole ride. However, his wife Sophia calmed him. She even made fun of him by calling him 'crybaby'. After coming back from the airport, the entire day Jack locked himself in Mia's room, he even left his dinner incomplete.

Sophia was not prepared for this. She knew Jack ardors his daughter the most in his life and it must be awfully painful for him. She is a mother, she's also miserable for her daughter and she love her too. She is also feeling lonesome but she had already agreed the fact that Mia required some freedom to make her life on her own and to take in the outside world. She and Jack will not forever be with her.

When we see from Father's POV, it is arduous for them to acknowledge the truth of his baby girl, initially grown up and shortly she will leave him. Many Fathers have gradually self-proclaimed that they undergo tremendous grief and wretchedness, when their girl child leave. It is not a surprising statement, we have overheard every now and then, how girls are so attached and devoted to their fathers and vice versa. Fathers always try to provide the best thing to their children and try to fulfill all the demand of theirs. They are also characterized as the best savior from mom's scolding. Many studies conducted revealed; men feel remorseful when they are unable to spent more time with their children because of lots of office work etc. but they also bury their affections and not once show it to others. The expression "Manly look" attach to their approaches shove them to control their tears. However, Women, who as a dutiful mother constantly near her children are less driven by the syndrome. Women display their affection faithfully and straightforwardly admit the actuality. I think, it's also doable since Women have undergone countless farewells in their existence; specifically, their marriage. However, men who are at all times enveloped by their closed one and certainly not have been separated, bears more pain.

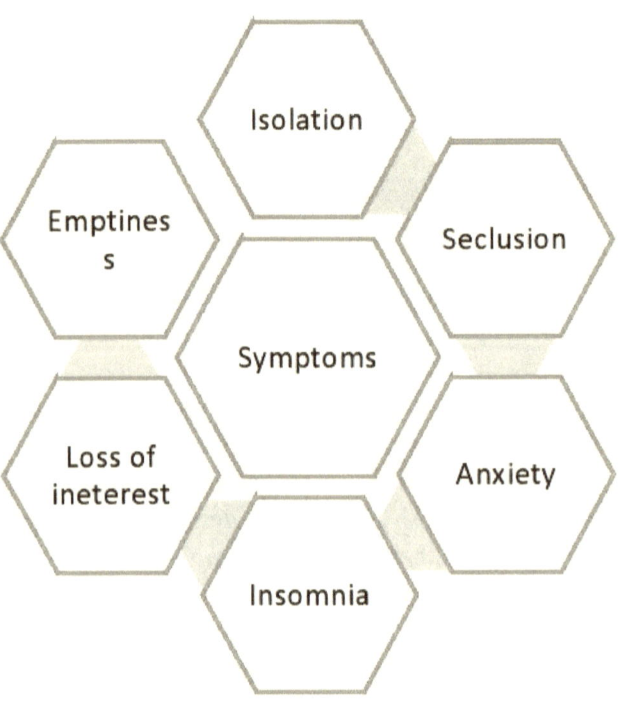

Womankind whose distinctiveness has been centered around the position of respectful Mother, it is not surprising to come across an extreme privation of individuality whilst priming for kids going away from home. They might realize themselves distrait that they haven't achieved beyond in lifespan, as mother universally emptied all their expectations, faiths and ambitions into the nurture and safeguard of the family. We all are acquainted with lifecycle. It goes on and change. But Empty Nest Syndrome is factual, and the escorted despair can be incapacitated, if controlled aptly. If somebody is powerless to discover the way out, you must go for therapy sessions and resolved your concerns.

Within Human development there is different stages - childhood, adolescence, adulthood, and old age. The empty nest syndrome influences and boomerang child phenomenon upon human existence are overwhelmingly observed. Once there are transmutations in human lifecycle and people stumble on newfound meaning of living, they come across an emotional variation. For motherhood, they move into the chapter of hollowness, after their single child or the smallest kid of the family leaves them. When we see around ourselves, we'll find, these days there is a shortage of jobs obtainable in the market. In such circumstances, numerous graduates who moved far away to study, once again they have to return home to reside with their parents. Returning home can be because of - relationship ending, financial drawbacks, sacked from the job etc. they are insinuated as boomerang teenager. Homecoming of adolescents to settle with their parents - the professed 'boomerang generation', trigger a noteworthy deterioration in parents' comfort zone and welfare.

A new solidity in the personal relationship of parents emerges and they find it satisfying during the freedom which they get from their children's away. They appreciate this period featuring in life, it gifts a conduit to finding new interests and liking. When their offspring come back, it is a desecration of stability in free life. Many surveys conducted revealed that it drives a pecuniary compression on parents, who are roughly around the age of 45 to 60. Instead of taking care of themselves at this age, their twisted life has to take care of kids. But further we can come up with a progressive clarification of all this. Possibly, children feel honorable in living with their parents and it develops a shrinkage in Generation gap. Conceivably the older people win over their age factor and confidentially don't demur this unremitting broadening in parentage.

" I cried a lot when my children left to academy. Indeed, I truly yearn for my kids.... it was the first time when they left so far and that too on their own to stay in different city..." Contrariwise, her grief was abridged as she revealed that: "…. a lot of office work, responsibilities of in-laws, taking care of pets.... kind of abetted me a lot in unchaining myself from misery.... made it tranquil to get ahead and live."

"...In spite of my office timings, i always drive my girl all the way down to college and make sure she is okay...

Customarily, human experienced an extreme loss expected from empty nest syndrome and accordingly, they need to give as good as they get through their optimistic fighting rather than deleterious response. The parents should be geared up for the parting; by crafting the headstrong accession which displays both the children and the parents are all set to move ahead.

CHAPTER III

Case 1

Kiran is a single mother. She lives in a small city Ranchi, India. When She turned 29, she chose to adopt two boys and never get hitched. She calls her son Luv and Kush. Both of them are now grownup and of same age. At present, she has reached the age of 65 and is retired. Both her son left her in her empty nest and lives in different towns, they are employed in some MNCs. They also compel her to live with them but she conveyed to live alone. Last year Kush also get wedded and set out living with her wife.

Kiran POV: I also now and again bear abandoned or desolate but I do not want to turn into a burden on my sons. One is newly wedded and it will not be the best decision to live with him. Although Luv lives in Delhi and I have stayed with him many times but I hate living in closed environment of Delhi. At least in Ranchi, I get fresh environment to breath in. It asphyxiates me to live in metropolitan cities. I enjoy to live in a place of open grounds, clear sky and less pollution. They always come to meet me on occasions like Diwali, Holi etc. It is sunniest day of my life meeting them.

Kush left home, when I was 55 years old. At that period, I was employed and my tiring life not once made me realised of the aloneness. After one year, Luv also left. I handled myself really well during those days too. In all honesty, those were the blissful moment of my life seeing my children grownup and standing on their feet.

But after the retirement, it made me realised of my remote or barren life. I have forever battled singlehandedly in taking care of both my sons and befall into a sole bread winner in a family. I have also a desire to live with my children but I can't. As a devoted sentinel, I played the best doable role of mother and father equally in their existence.

Nowadays, I have no yearning of being adept to grow into my personal empty nest without my kids. To dazed out of the confinement, I got a pet to aid myself in the position of ensconcing the brimming hollowness. Kiran come across a solution of her empty nest syndrome by petting a dog and it turns out to be the best decision for her.

16

CHAPTER IV

Case 2

Bill and Heerlen are couple of mid age. They live in New York. They have two daughters. One is married three years ago and another is engaged and staying with her fiancé, in same city. Bill and Heerlen are satisfied with their life and well-settled children; hence they make a decision to go on a world tour next month. The whole schedule of trip is premeditated. They are super energized about it. Being a prosecutor, Bill's life was very busy but he managed to handle his family proficiently shorn of any struggle. Now, he and his wife are looking forward this trip as a boon in their marriage life. Earlier, they never get free time from parenting two children and their careers. Now, is the best phase of their life. Heerlen is also proud of her accomplishments (dutiful mother and business woman) and when her kids left home, she felt a sense of relief. She gets retired at early age and started going out with friends and enjoying life. She also spent her time in planting and taking care of pets.

A week before the trip scheduled, their wedded daughter (Mia) showed up at their house with her loaded personal belongings requesting shelter from her shattered relationship with her husband. After clarification, they got to know that Mia is barren and her in-laws throw her out of the house, reasoning to it. They had also succeeded in making her sign the divorce paper. Both Bill and Heerlen are devasted listening the news and they embraced Mia whole-heartedly. Bill and Heerlen, had never expected their daughter to hide her problems from them. They think it is theirs fault they could not see the emerging difficulties in Mia's life.

As the life continues, emotional condition of both parents began growing critical. They reprimand themselves for their daughter's condition. Their own marriage existence started turning unhealthy. Now and then, they become aggressive on simple issues. The boomerang experience for them had turned awful. To come out of this situation both the parents and Mia have to find the solution on their own and if possible, they can look for counselling.

19

CHAPTER V

Case 3

Neeta is a 45-year-old divorced mother with one daughter. She lives in Lucknow, UP. She is a government employee. Her working hours are fixed from morning 10 to Evening 6. Because she was a divorcee, Neeta and her daughter were the only one who lived together. Neeta conceived Nakusha, during her countdown of Divorce. During those days, her becoming pregnant turned her devastated life in complete U shape. So, naturally, Mother and daughter were very close to each other. Neeta can't live without her daughter, Nakusha. When her 23-year-old daughter Nakusha left to complete her studies, then was the time, Neeta entered the empty nest phase. She was worried of her daughter safety and fearful of living alone in seclusion.

Every night, at dinner time, looking the vacant chair in front her made her to cry your eyes out in solitude. As the time goes, she understood, she as well needed some peaceful time to think about herself. She sealed the emptiness and counteracted her seclusion by enrolling herself in stitching classes and she spend her weekends with her friends. Despite the fact that, she anxious about her kid and long for Nakusha's presence in her house, she fathomed she is still has a long life to live and from time to time, she had to fight the battle to survive.

Neeta was adjusting to her newly made happy lifestyle and has just come out of Empty nest Syndrome, when her daughter boomeranged home. Nakusha returned back to her mother because she was unable to get job. Neeta was flustered over again due to transformations in life, nevertheless attuned herself to it and felt thankful and delighted to have her daughter back.

22

CHAPTER VI

Case 4

Ritika met the empty-nest stage with depression, anxiety and insomnia, when her youngest kid left her house. It gets nastiest, when she gets fired from the job after few weeks.

She had not even processed the news, when after few days she received a call from Karan, her firstborn son. He notified her, the blunder he had committed by making a girl pregnant out of wedlock. He liked her a lot and want to get married to her, as early as possible. Listening the news, Ritika felt deceived by her own blood and started doubting her upbringing. She felt pathetic and repents her motherly preaches.

Taken as a whole, it formed a hollow in her healthy life. To take her out from the abyss of darkness, her husband Laxman challenged her in many sorts, like- cooking competition, gardening, playing video-games etc. After few months, she opened a tutoring class at home and become a well-known tutor in her town. She even asks her maid to leave the job and started doing everything on her own. Her lifestyle completely changed from being a dispirited mother to a lighthearted and happy-go-lucky person. It was simply because of spousal support. If her husband would not have taken a step in making her come out of dejection, then today, her psychological strength along with her domestic life has been trashed. Whereas, the husband circumvented the battle of his by enclosing himself in his business and taking care of his wife.

24

CHAPTER VII

Something more

Caretaker protagonist: Together mother and father personate valuable and atypical protagonists in their children's life. The *"responsibilities"* of nurturing a baby are segregated uniformly amid both. But then again child-rearing is immeasurably ahead of many obligations. It emmeshes elevating child's welfare by strengthening overall considerations. The role of parents preponderated irrespective of their culture, traditions and background.

I was selected as a full-time nanny of Jack's children, when they were around 6-7-years age. He was a divorced when I first met him during the job interview. As the days passed, naturally I got closed to his children and they also started liking me. Due to which, Jack proposed me for marriage. I was elated plus sad because his parents and relatives were totally against this. They only see me as a brutal step-mother. But I always see them as my own.

"...uh...when my second kid left for job, I was very sad. There was a new shift in my life. I fear the loneliness at vacations. Then the demise of my husband Jack gave me an excessive emotional pain of wound carved in my heart. I am still worried about my kid's well-being. I am afraid they will leave me alone and I will never see them again. As I'm their step-mom, feeling of loss and abandonment always scare me.

Construing these grief-stricken statements, there is an imprint she even now longs for her children and will do anything adhering to the fostering responsibility regardless of her identity as a stepmother.

Different outlooks: This is linked to eclectic choice of sentiments connected to unalike personalities in the course of empty-nest disorder. It can be constructive or destructive. Optimistic discernment passes relief, enthusiasm, independence, or contentment noticing children's progress. When we perceive, the damaging edge, for several individuals it transforms their life and make it full of misery, mourning, desolation, rejection or lonesomeness.

"I'm glad ...my youngest kid too left overseas for job... It's the greatest moment in my life. I was constantly concerned for his career. He certainly not ever showed interest in studies and was counted an average student. When I heard the news of his selection in one of the best corporates In Hong Kong...I cried...uh...not of fear or concern but it was happy tears. I am not lonely or feel deserted living alone...I'm delighted seeing my children growing and achieving success."

Reverse married life:Having a kid undoubtedly makes your existence tiring, worrying and chaotic. Amongst all the work, staying with in-laws (esp. female), taking care of everyone's need and wants makes you workaholic. You never know, when the time flies and you are left alone. The kids will leave, those four walls become soundless and you have only relaxing time left in hand. In the hectic phase of twenty to thirty years, many a times we as a married human, we make many mistakes. Those faulty moments sometimes make our personal relationship to reach an end. The empty nest is the best time for them to reverse their married life and reach the happy stoppage.

"I was always busy in taking care of my children. I was so engrossed that i started overlooking few things and some are related to my married life. As the time resumes and both my kids started growing, the growth of my private life came to a halt.... My husband and I started fighting a lot. We never fight in front of children but behind the closed doors we argued a lot. The situation become so worst that Ben told me to give divorce."

This wasn't the life I had even once dreamed about. One day, Ben returned from office and asked me to go for counselling. The counselling sessions helps me a lot and my life are reversed in a new way.

Empty nest syndrome is never a medicinal illness, reasonably it is an emotional sensitivity. It has to be treated with love and care. Since beginning parents must understand the human life cycle linked with society. Having a firm mental status is fundamental prerequisite to handgrip or dodge the empty nest phase. To overcome the situation from starting keep your expectations limited from your kids. It helps in not becoming a victim of syndrome. Buy some space for yourself in your busy life of taking care of children and also give them space too. Accepting the reality help in making your life easier. Giving and taking space since beginning reduces the hollowness. These rough explanations and proposals made by me on the basis of my personal observation. There can be more and many other decisions to survive in the empty nest syndrome.

RASHMI SINHA

CHAPTER VIII

Midlife Blues

The word "midlife crisis" is portrayed as bedlam and unexpected modifications in individual objectives and standard of living, consequential to becoming old. It epitomizes a multifaceted interchange of atypical dynamics. Mid-life blues have a lot to do with Empty nest syndrome, Boomeranged generation, menopause and sandwich generation and at last career alterations and difficulties. The term "Mid-life crisis" came into existence in 1965, by Elliot Jaques. According to him, in the middle phase of natural lifecycle, there is a change when people turn from young to old. At some stage in, a few middle age people start gaging their accomplishments, failure, visions etc. According to our understanding, some men and women individually live through a midlife crisis. It is a period when people interrogate their standard of living and do the modification bestowing to their emotive prerequisites. Anyone can live through midlife crisis, even those who are born with silver spoon. I think when we become old, we face many changes – it can be related to career, our relationships, our passion, hobbies and dreams. It is a defined stage in lifecycle which reverse the thinking of individual in different ways. It has positive and negative side both.

Jemimah was a 40 years-old woman, living with her husband alone. Her children were married happily and living in different country. She and her husband were always busy in their work and spent less time with each other. She decided to give resignation and spent time at home being a housewife, she thinks she has given a lot to her career. It was her dream of becoming a journalist and she has grown into a great one but she started abhorring her job, and a lifetime staunchness becomes a mock. She has also turn alcoholic to mask her feelings of regret and depression.

Occasionally, individuals experiencing midlife crisis still do not believe the truth of concept. A midlife crisis may be the starting point of ending your private, emotional, and pecuniary permanence. A familiar warning sign of a midlife crisis set in motion with blame game crop up between couples, acquaintances or amid families. In this phase of life cycle, people are continuously perplexed of their willpowers and they denunciate their own children, parents or any other known person. They try to shelter themselves in a hollow by offending the sentiments of other. Their strength of mind become torpid. Eventually, the reason became divorce, career change or getting terminated, children leaving, death of parents etc. As a whole fear of changes in life triggers the loneliness and misery giving it a name called midlife crisis.

Blake was a 45-year-old guy, married happily to Jemimah. Meanwhile from last few months Jemimah observed, Blake has become miserable. It is not his nature, he was a cheerful person but since his father's demise few months back, he stopped showing interest in anything. She can state that he is going through a midlife crisis. Jemimah always try to cheer him up but he never showed any interest. His schedule was simple, going to office early in the morning, returning at 8:00 in the evening and after dinner he close himself in his room.

A number of people who undergo the crisis be subjected to depression, atypical hungriness, pessimistic opinion, failure to sense of purpose, be diagnosed with innumerable health problems. All these indicators impinge on their frame of mind and it can deleteriously influence their other good relations.

Mrs. Padma Roy is a 49 years old woman employed with a pharma company and is well recognized. She lives with his husband and in-laws. It is already been 14 years of their marriage and they do not have any children. Every time they go to a social gathering or block party, people sneer at them based on their age. Padma was informed of this that's why she has number of times asked Arun (His husband) for adoption. Listening the same thing every day, Arun started becoming grouchy which had never transpired in the past. He was always a positive person and never took heed on such matters.

Due to his changing attitude, his colleagues began to advise him that he is losing motivation and his productivity level has also decreased. He even received a letter from administration as a warning.

Regardless of all his endeavors, he was powerless to control over his depression. After 14 years into a relationship with Padma, Arun, opted to find a young girl of his choice and go for a divorce. He desired to live a happy life. He intended to show the society or his friends that he's still young and manly. In hopefulness to change his life style Arun began looking for a girl of his choice, who matching to him could be his future wife and he will soon become father of a child.

Many a times adults like Padma and Arun struggling to deal with a midlife crisis possibly will modify their preferences or way of life precipitously, comprehending the necessity for a novel intend and newfound impugns. Individuals enduring or living through a midlife crisis might roll up cantankerous or choleric shorn of rationalization. In appendage, they correspondingly express impetuous edicts. A midlife crisis may perhaps encompass out of the blue vicissitudes in veneer, containing uncommon approaches to change lifestyle. The adult undergoing through this might prerequisite to keep on appearing charismatic. Somebody walking through this lay siege to younger age bracket. Indicators of a midlife crisis might take account of the inner breakdown, dwindling motivation level.

After few days, in one of the societies gathering Arun met Anika. At the first glance, he found her jaunty and lively. Arun instantaneously liked Anika and make an effort to get her attention. Arun have confidence in finding a devoted mate in Anika.

Padma and Arun's parents were aware of his deed and they reprimand his action by talking to him. But Arun was rigid on his judgement. Starting few days were best for Arun and Anika, they started dating and Arun even hang with her younger friends. Slowly but surely Arun started to feel irreconcilable. He sensed that Anika is not the same, when she is with her friends of same age. He questioned her but the situation become worst and their relationship came to a halt.

In next to no time Arun again started to become petulant like the past days. This time his family asked him to go for counselling session.

A midlife crisis is frequently shelved as a shallow, outlandish condition. It turns out to be a stale joke of middle-aged group dating younger generation, or wearing unique dresses to impress others. But many people do suffer and they recognize that time has come and they are no longer the same good looking, energetic or motivated human being. Consequently, they can experience a low self-reliance/ self-confidence that crashes their existence and livelihoods.

How to solve midlife issues?

Women's POV

Mid life crisis is not about retrieving and attaining formative years (the past) but it is all about encountering newfangled ambitions and viewpoint in time. Womankind who are constantly standing in a row and running after the ambition go down, however females who are in default of any aspirations since beginning confront challenges at every stage and they surmount devoid of trepidation. There are discrete prospects of crisis. Time and again the duration of middle age summons adverse effect on body, mind and soul. People think it can be related to become old/maturity, heightened emotions, absentmindedness, Sex related complications in females, menstruations, empty nest syndrome, hopelessness and dejection. It also gives birth to suspicious deviations of mind, thought process and standard of living /habits. The transmutation phase in human body at mid age strikes amid the age bracket of 40 to 50, and it's a cycle of biopsychosocial renovations. Biologically thinking, it leaves a trail of great impact. Taking rational decisions turn out to be obligatory as they think there is less time accessible for them. An episode of insecurity or randomness in women's life undertake in the midlife (35 years age). It is a phase of emotional maturity, and the beginning of life calculation is boosted, they begin imagining or doubting their future. It gives a tie for self-evaluation to many females. Once they reach the age of 30, they start growing old and it became a reality for many. An entire new-fangled blueprint of future life in which there is presence of social control, mental potency, facades look fitness physical condition, communal adjudication, endowments and shift in notion come to life. Prominent objectives for women in midlife were refining connections with relatives and colleagues', well-wishers, taking care of sick in-laws, thinking of children future (studies, fees, marriage etc) and work out the financial prerequisite for old age.

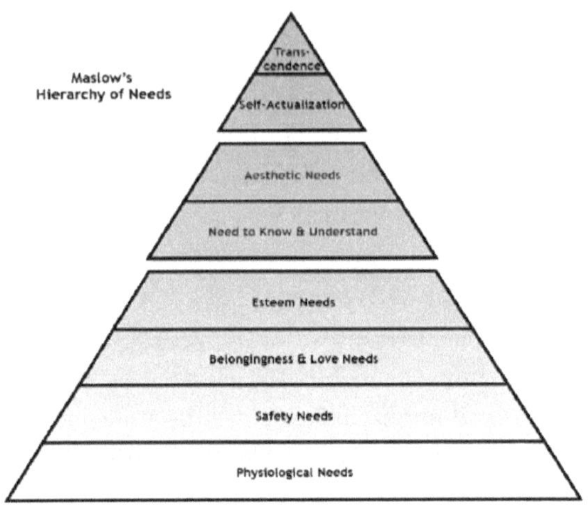

Womankind who raise through struggle and fulfill their needs (Maslow hierarchy)- they have one catchphrase to accomplish all in all. Reaching at certain age, when their body or mind become less competent, the precept of their life start creating restlessness inside, when they become incompetent to climb the ladder.

Rita is a 38 year-age-woman. She is a model by profession and has succeeded at very young age. When she started this profession, her dream was to grow into a well-known model internationally and she crave to work with top fashion industries. At the early phase, in her 20s, she earns fame and money undoubtedly owing to her diligence and uphill struggle.

But from last one year, she is confronting a lot of contests in workplace. She has to muddle through unending unfairness at workplace. To prove herself, she has to compete with new young models in the industry. With passing time, she had also lost the predilection of upholding herself. Her disenchantments had reduced her motivation level.

If you have arrived at this track and you are perplexed what do next? Where to go? What's in store for me in future? Do not get restless. Talk to your acquaintances or any reliable soul. If it is feasible, go for counselling session and discover your inner self. Equipped with this wisdom Women might recover the crisis and their adult life will be converted to bearable. The inborn starring role of women as a mother, daughter, sister and grandmother make the circumstances more judicious for them. Women psychological study is an inexact framework, which incorporates not only their innate responsibility but also highlights communal functions and the engagement they have in environs.

.... personal embitterment is time and again sink womenfolk down.

.... Women always keep themselves at last, when it comes to family, husband or children. In the whole shebang they put an effort to uncover self-esteem/ self-worth. They go all out to find an answer and they look with in themselves and condemn themselves before pointing fingers to others.

.... Many times, collective burden on females, makes them restive. Society always prove them weak. They question who they are? What they have to do? What they can't do? What

to wear? How to behave in public? and more. The term "Interrogative" is clipped by their title.

By convalescing your routine, countless deleterious symptoms can be mastered or transposed, in addition you can swapped a defining moment into a possibility for improvement. Nearly all Counselling professionals try to communicate a midlife crisis as a good fortune to detect your erstwhile engagement, reconsider your current and upcoming urgencies and revamp your existence into premium form. Foe many it is a refashioning episode, blotted by colossal escalation in the vicinity of winning newfangled intents or come flooding back to bygone days. It's correspondingly in connection with newborn goals and purpose in life. Women adults devote most of their free time fretting about their looks. For them, a young-looking concealment or façade is an essential care and they make a supreme effort to prepare themselves look babyish at mid age. Natural transformations in human body for instance getting wrinkles on face, hair turning white etc. make them lose sleep. Women start spending more time in spa taking care of facial attractiveness. They believe getting old is life threatening.

Men's POV

.... I want to give resignation.
..... I want divorce.
..... I should have become an engineer rather than becoming a doctor

All the above statements are made by middle age group men fall under 30-50 years age bracket. They sound dispirited or demoralized in their life. They appear as if they want to leave behind the whole thing and attain "Nirvana". Unsurprisingly, this behavior has an expected unfortunate bang on their personal relationship along with professional existence.

Henry is a 42 year-old-age man. He married his college girlfriend Natasha at the age of 25 and they are together since then. During the college days, they were the most popular couples in the entire university. He was head over heels in love with Natasha. Now reaching the age of 42, Henry again started craving the same popularity which he had earlier. Girls talking about his looks, clothes and all. He meditates upon what it would be like to have a new girlfriend again, a new partner in life to enjoy, and the same popularity like past.

This is not wisdom. Wise people do not marches becoming imprudent. They need to contemplate what is going on? What they are expecting? They need to talk to someone to clean up their mind. Contemplation and meditation empower them to have better consciousness of what is their life purpose and goals. Spontaneous pronouncements can ravage your time ahead. Men in middle age suspect they are miserably entombed in a character which they never wished for. They are more compelled when they have a burden of children, ailing parents and wife. Being the sole wage earner in the family, they had a heaviness over the head to break the chains and take off.

How to survive

Many people unfailingly justify to change their lives in improved version. This is what a fearful person does every time. People capitulate on the feet of nightmares and finally without fighting they give up their dreams. Fear is what trap them inside and they never allow them for self-actualization.

- *Work on your life goals*
- *Search the purpose of your life*
- *Do not think about past*
- *See happiness everywhere*
- *Exercise*
- *Keep yourself motivated*
- *Self-actualization and self-realization*
- *Support your dream/ find new dreams to fulfill*
- *Talk to people/ share your problem with spouse, friends, relatives*
- *opt for counselling*
- *Always be positive*

CHAPTER IX

Case 1

Raj is 49 years of age and has been living in South Korea for the past 30 years with his wife Natalie, his parents and a girl child. He is a software engineer employed with renowned company at topmost level. During his college days, he was an ambitious person, he enjoys visiting new places, Para mounting and he has also earned many awards in academics.

His daughter was born when he was 30 years old, and for the following 15 years subsequently, he was overjoyed to look after his daughter he had always wish for. He breathed a satisfyingly providential life.

...Oh, I was young! and also, physically fit during those days.

He aspired to take his daughter on vacations unconditionally the world over and he did without raising a question. He fulfilled all her demand. Attaining the age of adulthood one day his daughter also left him and moved overseas for higher studies. It was the worst day for Raj. He turned completely distressed but, in some way, he holds back by getting engaged to his work. Right now, reaching the age of 49, he believes he is going through a "Midlife crisis". He doesn't get an adequate amount of sleep as it should be and hc's always apprehensive about his father's death, which took place few months back. At the workplace as well, he is incapable to give proper attention. Many of his colleagues recommended him to go for psychotherapy.

"...my dad and I were relatively close. I miss him a lot. Without him i feel incomplete,"
"It hurt...hurt a lot"

The pain of loss submerges a midlife adult emanates with a stream of compassions and sympathies that possibly will catch hold of durations to settle down. People facing midlife crisis combat in conjunction with overshadowing nihilism.

Raj is hesitant to talk to his wife about his condition, hitherto the noticeable absence of interaction between the couples can turn out to be the foundation of the connubial complications. The psychotherapist also expended specific time debating with Raj how interaction can improve a bond between the couples. If they do not share their feelings, it can result in divorce or create negative impact on married life. He also illuminated that by speaking or sharing about one's uncertainties or teething troubles, worry and weaknesses can beyond doubt helps in coming out of depression.

Taking his recommendations, he began revealing the whole lot to his wife. It made Raj realised that increased interaction between the couples genuinely facilitate in lessening numerous of his complications. There is a mysterious side of countless complications in midlife crisis, which we are incapable to distinguish single-handedly. In such situations, we require a friend or companion in life to encounter them and get rid of them from our life.

1. What to do if your parent's demise stimuluses midlife crisis?
2. How justifiably you counter the conditions?
3. What are the approaches to get out of sensitive syndrome owing to mourning?

44

CHAPTER X

Case 2

Nalin is 50-year-old man married to Kiara. They have to look after of an old parent and growing two kids (One girl and a boy), individually with meaningful monetary needs. Nalin is a professor by profession and his income is not too good. Whereas Kiara is a housewife, which makes Nalin the sole earner. Every thing was going good in their life but unexpectedly it appears "Midlife crisis" pass in their life.

"...I don't know what to do? I have two kids one girl and a boy. My daughter has reached the age of marriage and my boy is still in final year of his studies. There is no other income from their side. I have to also take care of my old parents."

"How will I find the best groom for my daughter? Every family asks for dowry. (Presence in Indian society)"

"I also have to start saving for old times"

Due to the negative circumstances growing in his life, Nalin's behavior turned aggressive at home. Every time he talks foully with his wife and get annoyed simply. Occasionally he considers to leave everything and run away furtively. His behavior started steering a harmful effect on his health too. He also began consuming alcohol to overcome the tension. The feeling of disappointment always triggers his mind. He thinks he's unable to find the best groom for his daughter owing to financial instability, not able to take care of his parents in the best hospital and is unable to send his son to the best college.

"...I am incapable of taking care of my family", his voice cracked.

"I am disappointed of my life"

It is also true crisis in life can enter at any stage. But the age of 30-50 is the most crucial for many because during those days' reliabilities become more intense for every person. You have to take care of your parents, children, other family members reliant on you. Alongside, you also need to take care of monetary permanency for life time. Priorities revolutionize from time to time as we grow up and it is unto us how we cope with them. Pressures or anxieties multiply and opportunities start to melt away. Most of us are settle on by this age and it gets challenging to accomplish and even perceive another possibility. Be sure to have various alternatives lined up is an crucial stratagem for handling pressure.

1. What steps he need to take to solve his problems?

47

CHAPTER XI

Case 3

Kadar is a business man by profession. He on no account desired to opt business as an occupation but unluckily, he had to take care of his family business. And, "yes" the unfulfilled craving of undertaking a different ambition permanently strike him and made his life depressing. He had already reached the age of 50 and living with his wife. Both of his children are married happily and living in different cities with their respective partners.

"...Uh, I always wanted to become a sous-chef", he said mockingly. "But my parents choose my career path and I'm still walking on the road to the chosen one"

"I can't do this more. I'm sick and tired looking the same numbers day in, day out, running after profit and loss"

".... My wife believes, I'm going through midlife crisis and she recommended me to enroll for counselling sessions"

"...also.... seeing my friends successful running after their dreams made me overwhelm with jealousy."

When people like Kadar enter the age of midlife crisis, it may be easygoing for them to not recall how faraway they have reached in their line of business. Kadar began considering all his unfulfilled wishes and goals he had not achieved regardless of things which he had succeeded until this time. You may well have to take footsteps to do things another way in your life to come out of the depressive zone.

The best way for you at this stage of life cycle is note down the objectives or achievements you have acquire till now, it comforts you. Furthermore, it provides you with self-assurance to great extent. Individually, every person suffers differently in "midlife crisis". People should never compare their situation with others. Always try to reevaluate only your condition and take action based on your own judgement. Do not get influenced by others. If doable take support from counsellor.

1. As a counsellor, what is your suggestion to Kadar?

CHAPTER XII

Case 4

Hi, I'm Rina and I am 43 years old housewife. I am married and my husband is 45 years old. We have one kid and he live in Delhi, working in MNCs. Few months back, my husband asked me to split up. I don't know, what is wrong with him. His behavior towards me has completely changed after our son left. He all the time becomes maddened and yell at me.

I tried talking to him and he disclosed he's seeing one of his member of staff who is younger in age. He also expressed he's unsatisfied with me and craved to live like old days, when he was single. He even put objection in our relationship.

It's true that midlife crisis is an episode full of mistrust, skepticism and discomfort. It makes people's life uneasy. Once they mull over their life and they question "this is the genre of happiness in their life that they need". It's also uncomplicated to proclaim why there is a rise in divorce and increase in extra-marital affairs amongst the middle age people. Undoubtedly, when the individual undergoing through the restlessness and distress and always raise questions on his lifestyle and challenge to resolve it by running after young leisure activity, that unquestionably endangers your married life.

1.   What do you think Rina need to do?

52

CHAPTER XIII

Summary

In conclusion, we can only express, that every single human being who are going through any of the crisis in life must deal with the grounds of their unfortunate or calamitous emotional state and struggle to settle them to steer clear of spontaneous decisions. They must take into account that their own deleterious state of mind will constantly try to hold them back and the after-effects will be unfortunate for their scenic future. It is a proposal to always hold the exquisite moments of your life that makes you feel genuinely fortunate and all the time remain proud of your achievements. Be indebted to your empathetic acquaintances.

I know many people in their early midlife age bracket having a pessimistic thought process. They most of the times take irrational and spontaneous decisions, which ultimately generates a new problem in life. They also do not have a realization of the chapter "Midlife crisis" opened in their life. They pass on through "empty nest syndrome, menopause, financial midlife instability and career midlife crisis" taking irrational decisions. People have to make themselves prepared to cross this crisis successfully since beginning. They must understand it is a psychological condition and if not handled properly, it will affect them who are dependent on us.

So, instead of grumbling and fretting, take necessary steps. Like-

- Take help

- Counselling is the best solution
- Always be positive
- Set your goals
- Purpose of your life should be clear
- Take a break from your hectic life
- Improve your relationship with others